God's Saving Grace

Richard Rios

authorHOUSE®

AuthorHouse™
1663 Liberty Drive
Bloomington, IN 47403
www.authorhouse.com
Phone: 1 (800) 839-8640

Published by AuthorHouse   03/03/2016

ISBN: 978-1-4969-7091-6 (sc)
ISBN: 978-1-4969-7092-3 (e)

Library of Congress Control Number: 2015902521

Print information available on the last page.

Any people depicted in stock imagery provided by Thinkstock are models,
and such images are being used for illustrative purposes only.
Certain stock imagery © Thinkstock.

This book is printed on acid-free paper.

Contents

Behind the scenes

God is at work behind the scenes
Let me tell you what this means
He is working things out for the good of the ones who love him
Even if your situation may look dim
It may look bad now
But in the end you are going to be saying wow
He is the father all powerful
As his followers we need to be forever grateful
Father god I thank you for the good and the bad
God loves us all like a dad
My family is my motivation
Together we will face all these trails and tribulations
We will serve the lord of all creation
Because he is the one who delivers us from this evil temptation
Remember his thoughts
Are above your thoughts

Blessed

I am blessed
The lord gave me his best
I am grateful for everything his has done
Especially blessing me with 2 sons
They are the world to me
Help me to teach them to be
Godly and faithful men
And to show them that I'm their biggest fan
I pray that you help me to set a good example for them
And show them they are a priceless gem
Help us teach them right from wrong
And teach them good christian songs
I have been blessed
And my life is no longer a mess
Thank you lord
For I no longer feel ignored
You have blessed my life abundantly
And changed my life silently
I thank you for my many blessings
Help them when they are confessing
All their sins to you
Lord I pray that you be with them in all that they do
I am so happy when I see their big bright smile
Father God help them to live a blessed lifestyle

Bow down to you

I bow down to you
One day everyone in heaven, earth and under the earth will too
You are the king of kings
We are suppose to pray for our enemies
Father help them to see that one day they will bow down to you too
You are the lord of lords
Your word is sharper than any double edge sword
When we bow down to you we acknowledge
you are the lord the most high
God is the lord over all and that is something we cannot deny
I bow down to you
Cause I love you
But you loved me first
Even when I was cursed

Broken

Father God I come to you broken
Help us to not let your word go unspoken
Mold us into who you want us to be
Because one day we will all shout with glee
Father I will never forget that night
That you showed me your everlasting light
That night I prayed for you to show yourself to me
And oh God you opened my eyes to see
When I prayed I had doubt
But you took away all that doubt
When you showed me Jesus in my dream
That is how I knew I have been redeemed
I thought my life was about to end
But I didn't realize it was just about to begin
That moment Jesus washed away all my sin
Lord you bless me over and over again
For that I will remain faithful
Father god help me to stay humble and grateful

Brothers

We share a bond that cant be broken
Even when our final words are spoken
We have endured a lot
Through the different things that have brought us distraught
We have been blessed to watch each other grow old
I will always cherish the fact that I got to watch yalls life unfold
I wont ever forget the fun we had when we were small
All the time we spent outside playing ball
I hope I have been a blessing to yall as yall have been to me
Remember that nothing in life is free
Our hardships made us who we are today
So just trust in God and let him show y'all the way

Chains

The lord above broke my chains
He took away all my aches and pains
To some that sounds so insane
Like the situation between Abel and his brother Cain
He is father all powerful
God ever merciful
He can take away all of your hate and pain
Let go and let God brake them chains
When Paul was in chains
He said to live is Christ and to die is gain
Will you accept chains for your lord and savior
Or would you rebel with bad behavior
Now that these chains are broken
Its time that gods word is spoken
So the whole world can hear
That Jesus is alive and here

Chasing

I got caught up chasing them nickels and dimes
Now I am here writing rhymes
Father when I made that decision I put my faith in you
But a lot of these people look at me and say what are you going to do
My answer is simply God is going to take me where he wants me to go
I'm trying to put my life back together like a bunch of legos
By putting my faith in you I know that you
are going to bring something better
All these people judge but you are our life inspector
That is why we praise you
Because you are the one that makes everything in our lives new
When things look bad
You always show us something that makes us glad
I know you are going to show me what I need to do
Because all I need is to praise and serve you
I cant help but to frown
But Jesus says turn that frown upside down

Clear

I want to make something clear
This is what I want you to hear
You no longer have to live in fear
Jesus the savior of the world is here
I don't do this for me
I want to help you believe
That there is only one true king
That is why I sing
To glorify him
Because my life is no longer dim
Jesus can save you too
The love that he has for us is oh so true
God is so amazing
He is bigger than anything that your facing
You will no longer be deceived
Instead be received
By the most holy, gracious, loving savior
He is a God full of favor

Conviction

Father show conviction to us all
Because we all fall
We have done wrong
Help us to stay strong
Lucifer comes at us from all directions
Father God forgive us for our every imperfection
I give my life to you and ask that you lead us in the right direction
Help us to feel your conviction
All we have to do is repent
In doing that it is God that we represent
We need your help to do what is right
We need you to win this fight
Between evil and good
Father shine your light in every neighborhood

Dad

I cant put into words what you mean to me
But you always told me to be all I can be
I am going to do my best
And the Lord will take care of the rest
You raised me from a boy to a man
You have always been my biggest fan
You taught me how to live full of faith, love and integrity
Because of that I know your love is full of purity
You were always there telling me everything was going to be alright
Especially when times were hard and you would work all night
I wont ever forget some of your favorite words to me
Although sometimes you wondered what would become of me
You always said we can do anything we put our minds to
And that saying is O so true
You taught me how to provide
And that is how I survive
You're the best dad
Because you disciplined me when I was bad
When you disciplined me you said that it hurt you more that it hurt me
And now that I'm a dad that is something that I really see
I want to thank you for guidance
You always tried to help me advance
I don't tell you enough how much I love you
As I look at my life in a review
I see how much I'm blessed
Because you always tried to fulfill my request
You taught me to be grateful
You are my dad and for that I will always be thankful

Defeat

You may think you are beat
But if you are on Jesus team you wont go down in defeat
Let Jesus light shine
Because he is always in his prime
Ask our holy father for his help
He is bigger than the worst hand that you have been dealt
We are redeemed by the blood Jesus shed for you and me
He opened the eyes of the blind so they could see
Jesus is the one who sets us free
Father God I ask that you be our rock
Help us to open the door when you knock
We all have a purpose
Show us all that we are not worthless
Lord I thank you for your love and graciousness
Fill us full of your kindness
Help us to not be boastful
But to always be thankful
Help me to not be proud
But always sing your glorious sound
Help me to not be meek
Because you are strong in every area I am weak

Destiny

What is your destiny?
Where are you going to spend eternity?
Lord show me your plan
And help me to be your biggest fan
I know my eternal destiny
I know you are going to defeat the laws of gravity
When you call us home
To live for you in your beautiful home
Its sad to think what some will face
In that firry hot and humid place
God I thank you for your love and grace
I hope they see what they deprived themselves of
I know you are going to take me where you want me to go
And you will keep me straight and teach me everything I need to know
I just ask that you help me to be true
In everything that you tell me to do
As long as I believe
I will receive your promise to us all
As long as we believe you will not let us fall
That is why Jesus accepted those nails
To save us from our bad and unthoughtful deeds
So lord help us all to plant your seeds

Deliver

Lord deliver me from all the evil
Show me how to beat the devil
Fill me full of your love
And help me to rise like a dove
Take this temptation away
And help me to survive another day
Show me how to live a life like your son
And forgive me for all the bad that I've done
Lord help me to be all I can be
And open my eyes and help me see
Satan brings us more and more
But you tell us that you are here for the poor
Lord deliver us from all this hate, lies and lust
But giving you thanks is a must

Discipline

In 2 timothy chapter 1 verse 7
We hear about our prize possession
The spirit of power
That tells me that he gives us the spirit of love and self discipline
That is where our responsibilities begin
We should be able to choose right instead of wrong
It is good to praise and thank him through song
Father God I ask that you help us all choose right
So we don't feel guilty when we go to sleep at night

Distractions

There are too many distractions
Take a look around and you will see all these sinful attractions
In the mind is where the battle starts
I pray that Jesus light shine in the dark
See we have to stay focused
That way Satan don't get us with his hocus pocus
We need to keep our head in the bible
And live like Jesus disciple
Don't let these distractions get in your way
God is the one we need to obey
I'm telling you not to get distracted
But to only stay proactive
The enemy will try to distract you in every way
We are the ones that Satan is trying to dismay
Even Satan knows that the bible is so powerful
A lot of us don't know that the bible is very resourceful
I will no longer let these distractions get in my way
Because I want to hear what the bible has to say

Emotions

I keep my emotions all bottled up inside
Father God I realize that our hearts need to coincide
Father forgive me when I stumble
Lord help me to always stay humble
Lord remove all this anger I have inside
This is when the hurt and healer collide
I feel my heart changing
Oh God my life is rearranging
I know now its suppose to reflect you
God is the one who gives us our value
Father help me to do your will
Thank you father for healing us when we are ill

Enemy

The enemy comes to kill steal and destroy
He wants to steal our joy
He wants to kill us all
He wants to torture us like the apostle Paul
He wants to destroy you and me
He don't know that Jesus sets us free
Satan wants your whole family
Jesus died for us voluntarily
Satan fills us with temptation
Jesus gives us sanctification
The evil one try's to make us hate
But its through Jesus that we know our eternal fate
The enemy wants us to be full of greed
But god will fulfill you every need
Don't be full of anger
If you are your life is full of danger
Walk in gods love
Put your faith in the lord above
Satan wants us to be stressed
He wants us to stay depressed
You don't have to live this way
Because it's a new day
I now bow my head and pray
Father god let your light shine night and day

Everything

As I lay here
I know you are near
So lord I ask that you be everything
And that we be nothing
But help us bring glory to your precious name
Because I know without you my life would be full of shame
I know something is wrong
But just help me to praise you through this loving song
You are the king of all kings
It is from you we get our eternal wings
So we can soar like a beautiful white dove
Because one day we are going to rise above
All this anger and greed
Then you will fulfill our every need
But help us to live your way
And you will grant us another day

Failure

Oh lord I have failed you
Oh my what am I going to do
I'm not the man I need to be
But lord I ask that you wash my eyes to see
I feel so guilty
But I ask that you take that humility
And turn it into something good
As Jesus hung from that wood
He took that humility from me
So one day I would be free
From all my bad and evil deeds
And that day he will fulfill my every need

Father God

Father God
I know you are no fraud
But some people don't believe
But all I can do is fall to my knees and pray that you open their eyes to see
The things you are capable of
That you are the lord above
You brought me out of my misery
You have revealed the ultimate mystery
They don't know who you are
Because they are out there way to far
So lord I bow my head and pray
That you give me the right words to say
So you can brighten their day
So that they can have hope
Maybe one day they would have faith like the
woman that touched Jesus' cloak

Giving him praise

I put my hands in the air
Because its only fair
To give him the praise
God is the one worth living for these days
That is why I point to the sky
Jesus saves us when we die
Not born of a natural birth
He came to earth
To give us hope, love, and peace
One day he will come and raise the deceased
People say you cant do this and that
Jesus picks up in every area that we lack
They say you wont be successful
But to that I say I am thankful
Because these words are just motivation
Jesus opens the door for every situation

God

God is molding me
God is teaching me
God is opening my eyes to see
The things he has in store for me
He is teaching me how to be a Christian
He is showing me all of his qualifications
The first thing is a must
We need to live in love and not lust
God is giving us all the qualifications
We must love all the different denominations
He loves us all like his son
And he forgives all that we have done
Father God thank you for being so holy
Sometimes we feel so lonely
But we know you are there
Because you will not put more on us than we can bare

G-O-D
He sent his son to die for you and me
He created heaven and earth
He knew us way before our birth
He is the king of kings
He prepares us for whatever this world brings
God is worthy of our praise
We are the ones that are saved by his loving grace
G-O-D
That's the name we need to shout with glee
He knows what we need before we even ask
With his help we can conquer even the tallest task
God is the creator of all things
Through his son we all get new beginnings
You are my God
I love to listen to your music on my ipod
Your most holy word
Is the most powerful thing I have ever heard

God opens the doors

God has opened many doors for us
He has been there for us
Every step of the way
He is with us everyday
No matter how hard life is he is there
Showing us the clothes to wear
In Ephesians chapter six
We hear the real fix
He shows us the belt of truth
Jesus is living proof
He shows us the breastplate of righteousness
As he fills us with his gratefulness
He give us the helmet of salvation
Because he is the giver of all creation
Pick up your shield of faith
We know Jesus isn't no wraith
And always carry the sword of the spirit
Because if you believe in Jesus
Eternal life is what you will inherit

Gods will not mine

Don't be prideful
Don't be boastful
Or you will feel Gods wrath
He gives you everything you have
God gives you no more than you can handle
We are not worthy to touch Jesus sandal
If you put your faith in him good things will come
When you do that you no longer feel numb
Everything that God does for us is for his glory
He shows us this through Joseph's story
There is no problem that is too large
Christ is in charge
God is there all the time
Everything happens in Gods time
Let others see Jesus in you
Rejoice in good and bad times because God is molding, and teaching you
Sometimes it may look like God forgot you
We need to learn that he doesn't change his mind
God made you like no other, you're one of a kind

Good news

Lord help me to spread your good news
And I want to thank you for paying my dues
For my wicked sins
But in the end you're the one that wins
You have paid the price for us all
Now its up to us to answer your call
All we have to do is believe
And you will be there when we grieve
Help us to live a life full of hope, peace and love
And help us to rise above
Help me to tell people about you
And all the things you can help them do
Help these people believe
So they will no longer be deceived

Grace

He saves us by his grace
He don't judge us by our race
He gives to us unconditionally
We need to receive it thankfully
He is the one that took our place
So don't let your life be a waste
Through his grace he has freed us all
Even through all the bad that we recall
He loves you so
That may be something you don't even know
He is the one and only savior
He is not a heartbreaker

Happy

I'm so happy
Satan no longer makes me feel crappy
Jesus is the lord over my life
I no longer have to face this worldly strife
Its God that fills me full of happiness
Because he fills my life with graciousness
He gives me everlasting peace
My blessings in life are starting to increase
When I let him take control everything started going good
The love he has for us is something that needs to be understood
I always use to worry
I now say I am sorry
I should have gave everything to him a long time ago
His unconditional love is something we cant out grow
God will no longer let you be unhappy
I promise if you turn you life over to our lord
You are the one that will reap the reward
That's why I will always be happy

Hatin

As I set here with these people hatin
I wonder why I am waitin
For these people don't know me
For the lord delivers me
From all that they hate
Because I am not taking satans bait
I just want to tell them
All about him
And give God all the glory
Because he ended my horror story
Jesus died for us
So why do we fuss
When things don't go our way
Because being able to praise him should make our day
For God sent his only son
So his will would be done
Why these people hate
Because that can keep them from the pearly gate
Jesus died for our sins
So one day we could eat in his fathers din
So when people hate
Don't take satans bait
Pray that the lord helps you
When people criticize everything that you do

Highway to holiness

Highway to holiness
We should live a life of gentleness
In Isaiah chapter 35 verse 8
God tells us he will make a fool walk straight
We all are like Simon Peter
But God has called us all to be a leader
We all mess up
But God is calling us to step up
Jesus came to earth to save us from our unrighteousness
We need to ask god for his graciousness
God is talking to you do you hear him
He will do miracles for you if you trust in him
Do you know who to call when you are in trouble
We need to live for our savior and stay humble
Its not what you know its who you know
Will you let god be your super hero
The lord wants our full attention
If you believe in him he will bring you divine intervention
Cry out to the lord during your distress
He can bring good out of your mess

Hope

Father God thank you for giving me hope
I often think about the times you could have said nope
God our father I ask that you make all this bad flee
Putting our trust in you is the key
Help us to trust you
And thank you for everything you do
You give us everything we need
You are the lord over all indeed
You will be blessed double
For all of your trouble
He took a man named Saul
And turned him into the apostle Paul
God is the one in control
I pray that we are with our God when they read the 7 scrolls

I believe

We all suffer from depression
Lord here is my confession
I don't believe in a religion
I believe in your conviction
I don't believe in putting someone as high as you
Because they cant do the things that you can do
They are only human
Some people don't know that we all face persecution
I believe
That Jesus died for me
I believe in the God head 3 in one
The father, spirit and the son
I believe that Jesus rose up 3 days later
There is no king that is greater
I believe god is real
Someday before him we will all kneel
I believe what the bible tells me
That if I accept and believe in Jesus I will live for eternity

I will not go down in defeat

Satan I will not go down in defeat
Because I'm going to be all I can be
The blood of Jesus will set me free
That is what opened my eyes and allowed me to see
Satan you cannot defeat us
So you may as well quit all that fuss
It is said that when two or more are gathered in my name I am there too
That means that there is nothing Satan can do
He tempts us at our weakest points
But God is the one that anoints
His word is sharper than any double edged sword
He is the maker of heaven and earth that is why he is my lord
As long as God is with us
No one or nothing can defeat us
He is the lord of lords and the king of kings
God will defeat everything that this world brings

Isaiah

God has blessed us to have you
And I promise we will be there in everything you do
I love to hear you laugh
I pledge to you I will lead you in the right path
Yall bring me so much joy
I tell you to live life and enjoy it
I want to tell you to make God first
And he will quench your every thirst
He is the maker of the heaven and earth
Without him your mom wouldn't have been able to give your birth
Love him and obey all his laws
And I promise you, your life wont have any flaws
I love you son
Even if your life has just begun

Jason

I want you to know how much you mean to me
I thank God for you because when you were
born he opened my eyes to see
You bring me so much joy
I'm sorry I can't buy you every toy
But I try to give you more than I had
Even when you have been bad
I want you to know that I am here for you
And you can do anything that you put your mind too
I love you to hear you sing all them gospel songs
But I am here to tell you to learn from all your wrongs
I want to help you answer your call
I will be there to catch you when you fall
You are such a wonderful loving and caring big brother
That is a bond that wont be broken by any other
We are not guaranteed another day
So always enjoy yourself and play
I love you more than life itself
You should always love your neighbor as yourself
In life you are off to a awesome start
Because no matter what anyone says you are so smart
I can only pray that God continues to grow your faith
Because you know that God has the power to keep you safe
I love you more than words can ever say
Always thank the Lord for giving you another day

/

Jesus

His name is Jesus
He is the one that saves us
He saves us from our wicked ways
We should give him all the praise
What's his name
He came to save the lame
His name is Jesus
He said he will never leave us
J-E-S-U-S
He will always give you his best
What his name
He don't want all that fame
Because he was put to shame
For me and you
So what are you going to do
Are you going to accept Jesus
He just may leave you speechless

Jesus paid the price

Satan is after me
But Jesus paid my fee
When he died on that old rugged cross
That gives him the right to be my boss
We want to be in control
But we just need to play our role
And Jesus will take care of the rest
Because he always gives us his best
We need to give it all to him
Especially when we sing that glorious hymn
Jesus is the one who sets us free
He is also the one who fills us with glee
Satan don't know that we play for the winning team
Because through Jesus we are redeemed
I'm not running from Satan no more
As long as God is with us we will always win the war
That starts in our mind
That is when we choose to be kind
I pray that God is everything
And we are nothing

Life

This life isn't for me
Thank you lord for opening my eyes to see
What is most important in life
That is my God, and my family including my wife
Lord I am so thankful to be home
And not be on the road all alone
I ask that you open the door
And help me to not be negative anymore
Help me to live this life full of faith peace and love
And to rise high above like a beautiful dove
I don't want to live for me I want to live for
the most holy and righteous god
Everything I do I want to be fruitful and pure that
way everyone will know you are no fraud

Look at the father

Set your eyes on the lord and everything else wont bother
Lift up your head and look at the father
It don't matter what this world tells you to do
Jesus came to die for me and you
Father God help us to stand strong and stay obedient to you
God is the giver of all hope
So when thing get bad put your faith in the lord and don't mope
Things aren't always as they seem
God will help you overcome satans scheme
The lord knows your heart
Accepting Jesus is when your life starts
What did Jesus think of you when you were at your worst
He still loved you when you were cursed
God loved us even when we were rebellious
We need to be more selfless
We need to bring victory to our family
Make God your foundation and your heart won't weigh so heavily
Many people have different points of view
But the word of God will always be true
No weapon formed against God's people will prosper
Jesus is the one that we need to imposter
We are not worthy of being in Gods presence
God needs to be our dependence
We are all sinners saved by gods loving grace
Remember on that old rugged cross Jesus took our place

Lord help me

Lord help me to be obedient to you
Help me to glorify you in all I do
I want to bring all the glory to your holy name
Because you endured all that hate and shame
So I can live the happy life
But help me when I face strife
Because Satan wants to steal all my happiness
But he don't know about your holiness
Help me to fulfill your purpose
Because no one knows what happens below the surface
Lord I don't want to burn in hell
I want your help when I fail
Lord catch me when I fall
And help me to answer your call
Help me to live with your love
And with peace from above
Help me to forgive like you
While Ill show people your true
For in the darkest hour
You will show your mighty power
And dismiss Satan sinners
With God's true winners

Lord

Lord how can I tell people about you
And all that you do
Open their ears so they can hear
And they can seek you and have now fear
Show them all your wonderful deeds
And maybe they will let you fulfill their every need
Open their eyes to see
And show them that you already paid their fee
Lord please help these people believe
That Mary was a virgin when Jesus was conceived

Lost

I was once lost
I would please myself at all cost
Until I accepted you as my lord and savior
Then I had to change all my wild and crazy behavior
Father God you changed me
You washed my eyes so I could see
I can do all things through Christ who gives me strength
That's in Philippians chapter 4 in the 13ᵗʰ verse
See that tells me he is God all powerful
So we should be so grateful
Jesus saved my soul
He tells us we will reap what we sow
God found us when we were lost
But Jesus is why we have Pentecost
I tell you that Jesus loves you
And he died so he could make you new

Love

Father God you love us so
I am more thankful than you will ever know
Some people don't understand
How you created the world and man
The answer is oh so simple
With god all things are possible
Jesus loves you so
The bible tells you so
Father god I'm sick of it all
I can only pray that you help me answer my call
Help me to lay down my life for you
Do with me whatever you so choose
I'm sick of all the lies
I guess its time to cut them ties

Loves ones

To the ones I love
I try to love you like the lord above
He gives us all the power
As long as we stand with him we are as tall as a tower
He loves me and you
God is with us in all we do
We need to give him all the glory
Because he is the one who writes this story
He loves us so much he gave us salvation
Through his greatest creation
He has blessed us all
He still loves us when we fall
So I say to you to live in love
And he will send his spirit upon you like a dove
Satan wants you to love this world and the things in it
But I am here to tell you that God loves you more than anything in it
So don't let these people places and things get you down
Because their are people laughing at your frown
Instead show them compassion
Because they may not know Gods fashion
He loves us all no matter what we look like
He even loves the things we dislike
His word tell us we should love our neighbors as ourselves
So lets lift up Gods word off that bookshelf
Because in it, it says God is love
So if we want to show people God we need to show them love
I love you all
So please answer gods call

Mind

I got a lot on my mind
Without my God my eyes are blind
Father God please take away all this stress
I know that I have been very blessed
Lord you have blessed me with more than I have ever asked for
But as I take a look back how can I ask for more and more
Just when I thought everything was back on track
Something happens and I get pushed to the back of the pack
Father help me to be strong
Because you are going to make right out of my wrongs
We are never promised tomorrow
I make Jesus Christ my hero

MOM

We have had some good and bad times
But we are going to reminisce as I write this rhyme
The main thing I love about you is your heart
Especially when you would push me in the shopping cart
God has a plan for us all
But sometimes we have to take a fall
I know now you see the light
Because Gods unconditional love is so bright
I know that you love your boys
Even though you couldn't buy us all are toys
You have always been there when I needed someone to talk to
I catch myself wondering without God what would I do
We both know that he has a plan
Because without him I wouldn't be a man
He shows us the way
And he is the one that allows us to live another day
I want you to know
That you will be your biggest foe
I remember when you were in the kitchen fixing us a hot plate
I can only pray that we will all enter that beautiful pearl gate
We have all done wrong
I got to tell you it makes my day to hear Jason sing that gospel song
And our newest baby boy
When he laughs he brings me great joy
Just remember in everything you do the truth will set you free
And if you put your faith in the lord he will open your eyes to see

Peace

We are out here searching for peace
For that to happen all the hate, anger, lust and greed needs to cease
Peace is something so great to feel inside
I am so tired of watching the news and hearing about another homicide
Peace is that this world needs
Follow Jesus he don't mislead
Peace is what people are looking for
If peace is what you are looking for turn to Gods word and look no more
When I found Gods peace in my life
It reminded me how much I needed Jesus in my everyday life
Peace is something we need to feel always
The best way to feel at peace is to study Gods word everyday
It works for me and it can work for you too
Its sad to think that some people don't even have a clue
Remember everything the devil tells you is untrue

Redeemed

I am redeemed by Jesus blood
Father God help my life not to be a dud
There is no devil in hell
That can redeem you like Jesus did when he accepted those nails
I will be the head and not the tail
Someone can tell the evil one my soul isn't for sell
Because I have been washed clean
Giving him glory thanks and praise needs to be part of our daily routine
It's the blood of Jesus that sets us free
I was once blind but now I see
So we can be all we can be
He paid for our soul with his blood
Jesus is our lifeblood
Its through Jesus that we are redeemed
So no matter how hard things may seem
Remember that Jesus loves you unconditionally
We need to tell other about Jesus more consistently

Sad

This world is getting so bad
Everything you see and hear is so sad
But let me tell you something good
This is something that shouldn't be misunderstood
His name is Jesus, he is the Christ
The people that don't know him are deprived
He entered this world and lived a perfect life
Then he died to save us from all this strife
He came to save us from all this strife
He came to save us all from all of our bad
We should love him and his father like a dad
Because he is the one and only lord
That is why peter cut that servant with his sword

Sin

Here we go again
I ask you lord to help me turn away from my sin
Its so hard to face all this temptation
But you can help me because you are the lord over all creation
I can only hope and pray that you show me the way
Please help me in everything that I say
I know that I have done wrong
Help me to live with you and stand strong
I declare you the lord over my life
I need your help to not get caught in that nightlife

Sins

What are you going to choose heaven or hell
God has something he wants me to tell
He is still alive
If you accept him you will have eternal life
Father help this whole world to see your grace
We need to see your beautiful face
I pray that someday they will believe
So we will all be received
Father God we are all in need of you
The lord is searching for me and you
He gives you double
For all your shame and trouble
All of our sins cause us destruction
Through Jesus we receive reconciliation
Father help us to stand for what is right
Because one day all of our sins will be brought to light
Lord no matter what you do
We cant hide from you
Father forgive us for all the bad we do
God showed his love for us while we were sinners
We should all become repenters

Special

You are special to me
Without you I wonder where I would be
I am glad you are mine
As long as we keep our faith we will be fine
You have given me all I can ask for
Your love is enough I don't need nothing more
Every time I look at our kids, they remind me of you
And all the wonderful things you do
To please us all
I thank God that he catches us when we fall
You are a wonderful mother
You are special to me and I don't need to go any further
You make me proud
Because what I have found
In you, you are so strong
I love to hear you sing your favorite song
I will love you forever
And will be with you in everything you endeavor
What god puts together let no man tear apart
With that said you will always be in my heart

Story

We all have a story to tell
At one point in our lives we have all failed
This is my story he want me to tell
I was living a life headed straight to hell
At one point I didn't believe
Because I was so deceived
But one night I was about thirteen
Little did I know Jesus was about to intervene
That night I laid in my bed and prayed for God to show himself to me
Oh boy did he open my eyes to see
Then I closed my eyes and had a dream
I suddenly awoke full of tears because I knew I needed to be redeemed
I remember that dream plan as day
I was so amazed not one word I could say
See I dreamed Jesus stood at the foot of my bed
I don't remember exactly what he said
But I knew then that he was real
I cant explain how that made me feel
At that time in my life I was full of anger and hate
But God showed me that his love was great
I woke up from his dream crying because I had been very bad
And that moment I knew that I hurt Jesus and he was sad

Thankful

I am thankful for my wonderful dad
Because he was there for me when I was bad
I'm thankful for our beautiful boys
In my life they fulfill it with all the joys
I am thankful for having such a loving and caring wife
I know that as long as God is our rock we can face any strife
I'm thankful for my grandpa
He always tried to catch me when I fall
Grandmas I will always be thankful for you
You encouraged me in everything I tried to do
I am thankful for all of my family
That God has allowed to grow so rapidly
To my wonderful and special brothers
I am thankful for yall we share a bond that cant be broken by any other
Most importantly I am thankful for our awesome God
The one who grants our final applaud

The ultimate seeker

God seeks us all the time
Even when we are not in our prime
But do we seek him the way he seeks us
Going to church is a plus
We don't need to stop there
Because he seeks us everywhere
He wants a relationship with me and you
So I ask what are you going to do
Are you going to seek him back
If you put your faith in him, he will take care of you in every area you lack
God is looking for us everywhere
So watch what you do and don't swear
Are you going to call out to him
Jesus tell us no one comes to the father, but through him
So if we seek Jesus we seek our maker
Seek him because he is the most holy peacemaker

Thinking

He tells me he cant stop thinking
That is why he isn't sleeping
I tell him to let go and let God
Because he isn't no fraud
He loves you and gave his only son
So you could live and have fun
Put your faith in him
And I promise he will not make your life dim
When you feel pressured from the outside
Stop and take a look on the inside
Its just a matter of time
Before he shows you that miraculous sign
Because he has great power
We don't know when is our final hour
So just give your life to him
When he is done he will show you the film
He will take all your thoughts
And put them in the right slots

Trials

We must go through these trials and tribulations
To meet our faithful obligations
To the one and only holy one
He is the one that delivers us from all the wrong we have done
We face trials and tribulations
Because Jesus is the author of our salvation
So father from above
I ask that you comfort us with your unconditional love
You are the only one that can help us in these times
Lord I ask that you help us not to commit these crimes
We are living in our last days
Father God protect us from these evil ways
Free us from all this commotion
Cause its getting harder to control my emotions
Its through the hard times that our faith grows
Help us to not be like the one who denied Jesus
3 times before the rooster crows
I cant face these times without my God
For what Jesus did I will always applaud

Truth

What's so hard about telling the truth
The bible tell us we need to be foolproof
I wonder why
People want to lie
Through these lies many people are deceived
To the truth they are deceased
Father God open there eyes to see
That the truth is what sets them free
When someone lies to me
I tell Satan in the name of Jesus he has to flee
I pray for the people that these lies deceive
The truth is what they will receive
Don't get me wrong I told my share of lies
Now that I am wiser I realize
How important it is to tell the truth
Often times telling a lie is just a excuse
To some people being honest is so hard
These are the kind of people we need to disregard
You will be free if you rest in the truth
Look at jesus he is living proof

Why

I often ask why oh lord why
God is the lord the most high
We need to live life for the most high king
And be prepared for whatever this world brings
Put your faith in God all powerful
We need to be more prayerful
God can do anything in your life if you ask
The lord can conquer the tallest task
Father God help us with the things we can't control
Accept Jesus as your lord and savior and he will save your soul
Often time we don't want to leave our comfort zone
If your not careful you may be there all alone
God put you where you are for a reason
So follow him and he will bless you in every season
His plans for our life is way higher than our own
One day you will be rewarded for every seed you sown

Wonder

Sometimes I start to wonder where I would be
If I wouldn't have realized that Jesus loved me
See when I was younger I was always mad
At that time in my life I didn't know that it made Jesus sad
I often said why would God do this to me
But I know that I went through them trials so I would believe
I wonder where I would be if I made better decisions
But really I believe that the lord would still win the competition
Because he is in control of everything
It took me a long time to realize that he is always forgiving
He forgives me and you
He is with us in all that we do
I made a lot of mistakes
In those times the lord showed me what it takes
Hard work perseverance and dedication
God can do anything but he likes our participation

World

What is this world coming to
Oh lord without you what would I do
This world is so corrupt
Help us to obey and not disrupt
Help us to just be in this world
And not of this world
This world is full of hate
But help us to fulfill our fate
This world is so bad
That is so sad
But from every bad you bring good
So every sad is understood
In this world are a lot of lost and lonely people
Lord help us to be your disciple
Help us to tell these people in this world about you
And to give all the praise and thanks to you

You

Everything I say and do
I want it to reflect you
Jesus gives us a holy life to pursue
Everything that I say and do
I want it to point to you
God I want you to shine in me and make me new
Father God help me to share your love
So people will believe you are the lord above
Lord Jesus help me to show your grace
So one day we will see your glorious face
Lord help me express you gentleness
So some day everyone will see your faithfulness
Father fill us with your everlasting peace
God I ask that you be my family's centerpiece
Lord I want to lead your people to you
The only way I know to do that is trying to be just like you
By doing that everything I say and so
Just needs to reflect you